WYOMING

A Turner Educational Services, Inc. book. Based on the Portrait of America television series created by R.E. (Ted) Turner.

Library of Congress Number: 87-16442

4 5 6 7 8 9 10   99 98 97 96 95 94 93 92 91 90

Library of Congress Cataloging in Publication Data

Thompson, Kathleen.
  Wyoming.

  (Portrait of America)
  "A Turner book."
  Summary: Discusses the history, economy, culture, and future of Wyoming. Also includes a state chronology, pertinent statistics, and maps.
    1. Wyoming—Juvenile literature. [1. Wyoming]
I. Title. II. Series: Thompson, Kathleen.
Portrait of America.
F761.3.T48   1987   978.7   87-16442
ISBN 0-86514-460-5 (lib. bdg.)
ISBN 0-86514-535-0 (softcover)

Cover Photo: The Wyoming Travel Commission

★ ★ ★ ★ ★
Portrait of AMERICA

WYOMING

Kathleen Thompson

A TURNER BOOK
RAINTREE PUBLISHERS

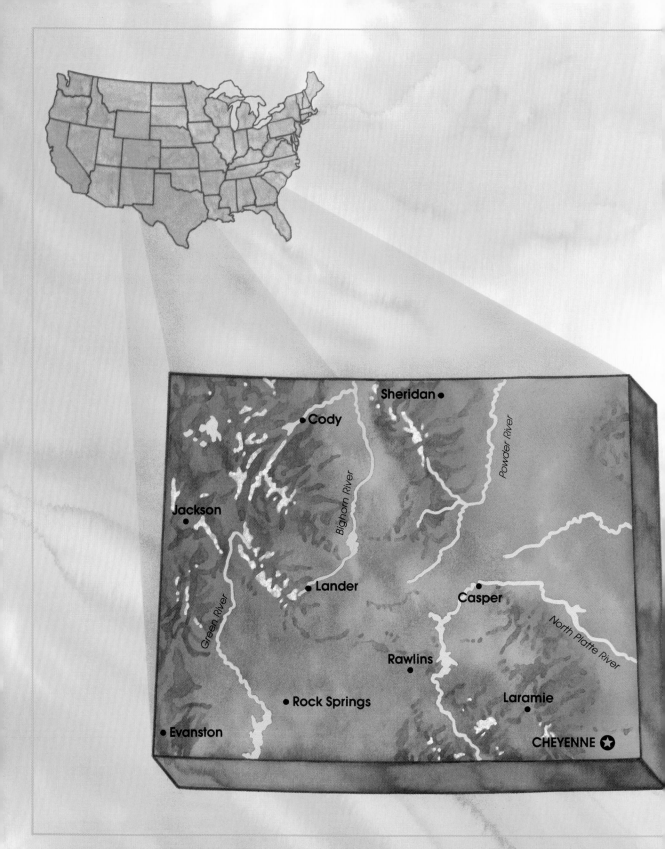

CONTENTS

Introduction   7

Home on the Range   9
  A Wyoming Childhood   20
  Lost Springs Wins   24

The Rich Earth   27
  A Big Job   30

Art West   35
  From Mountains to Mountains   38

Beautifully Slow   43
  Important Historical Events in Wyoming   45
  Wyoming Almanac   46
  Places to Visit/Annual Events   46
  Map of Wyoming Counties   47
  Index   48

Introduction

Wyoming, the Equality State.

"Get up in the morning before daylight and goin' out and catchin' a horse and listenin' to him nicker. And before the sun comes up, gettin' on him in the frosty air . . . That's why I live in this country."

Wyoming: cattle, timber, oil, mountains, minerals, and Yellowstone National Park.

"The people were so nice. Everybody was coming from everywhere and we were kind of all in the same boat and working toward the same end."

Wyoming is a place where cowboys still ride tall in the saddle. There is still room to breathe. Wyoming is the West.

The Grand Tetons, viewed from Taggart Lake.

Home on the Range

It was the home of the Sioux, the Arapaho, the Crow, the Blackfeet, the Bannock, the Cheyenne, the Shoshone. On the Great Plains among the tall grasses, the Indians hunted buffalo. In the Bighorn Mountains, they trapped beaver. But soon all that would change. Soon a different kind of people would come to tame the wilderness the Indians had loved, respected, and lived with for so long.

Legend says that Spanish explorers traveled as far north as Wyoming, but historians can find no evidence that the legends are true. Two brothers named Vérendrye ranged up from North Dakota in about 1742 and they may have reached Wyoming. Their journals are too confusing for us to know for sure. Meriwether Lewis and William Clark passed by Wyoming on

Bison in Yellowstone National Park.

their famous journey, guided by the Shoshone woman, Sacagawea.

And then, in 1807, a member of the Lewis and Clark expedition named John Colter left the group. On his way back across the continent, Colter set out into the Wyoming wilderness to do some trapping. He crossed the Continental Divide at Union Pass and finally found his way to Yellowstone Park. It's impossible to imagine what John Colter felt as he walked alone through the fossil forests, stood before the black glass mountain, watched the hot springs steam and the geysers erupt. He had discovered one of the most astonishing natural wonderlands the world has to offer. He was seeing a miraculous world no white person had ever seen before.

A few years later, the Wilson Hunt Price expedition passed through Wyoming on its way to Idaho. Because they were hired by John Jacob Astor of the American Fur Company, these fifty or

Lewis and Clark are shown with Sacagawea, the Shoshone Indian woman who guided them.

sixty fur traders were called the Astorians. In 1812, some of that party, led by Robert Stuart, returned through Wyoming. They discovered the South Pass and built the first European-style building in Wyoming.

Soon, fur traders and trappers began to find their way in numbers to this beautiful wilderness of the north. William Ashley of the Rocky Mountain Fur Company advertised for men to come to the Wyoming country. He created the fur traders' rendezvous. The rendezvous was a place where the company's pack trains brought supplies to trade for furs. It was also the great social event of the frontier. The rendezvous was a fair where Indians, trappers, and traders met to drink, dance, tell each other stories, and generally ease the loneliness of a mountain man's life. It was at the Grand Rendezvous on the Green River in 1835 that the Reverend Samuel Parker preached the first Protestant sermon in the Rockies.

In 1824, the Rocky Mountain Fur Company men started using the South Pass as a way through the mountains. The path from the

An early color photograph of geysers at Yellowstone National Park.

South Pass south across Wyoming through Bridger Pass eventually became known as the Overland Trail. It was a way to get through the Rocky Mountains without having to climb them.

Ten years later, Robert Campbell and William Sublette built Fort Laramie at the point where the Platte and Laramie rivers cross. They sold it to the American Fur Company, and it became the first permanent white settlement in Wyoming. Later, the U.S. government bought Fort Laramie and turned it into a military post.

The traders and trappers got along well with the Indians. They had no interest in trying to take the Indians' land away. But soon other whites would come into Wyoming and things would change.

It was a pair of Methodist missionaries, Jason and Daniel Lee, who opened what was then called the Oregon Country to farming. They traveled across the Oregon

Fort Laramie was the site of treaty councils between Indian tribes and the U.S. government.

Trail and were followed by others from further east who were looking for new homes and farms. In 1843, Marcus Whitman led the first great train of settlers over the trail.

John C. Frémont led a government expedition into the area in 1842 and reported back that the West was not a barren wilderness but a land of opportunity. Ten thousand copies of his report were published. In 1847, Brigham Young led crowds of Mormons along the Oregon Trail through Wyoming to Utah. When gold was discovered in California in 1849, thousands of "Forty-Niners" followed the trail on their way to find their fortunes in the gold mines.

In the years that followed, the Oregon Trail was the path of stage and mail coaches, the Pony Express, and the telegraph. In a sense, it was the Oregon Trail that opened up the West.

Not everyone was happy about this new path to the frontier, however. The people whose land it crossed—the Indians—were very angry. And they did more than complain. They attacked the wagons and stagecoaches that traveled along the Oregon Trail. Finally, the stage line was moved south to the Overland Trail, and soldiers were sent out to protect the white settlers.

The Great Treaty Council of 1851 was supposed to make peace between whites and Indians. But

Brigham Young led his Mormon followers west along the Oregon Trail.

the treaties were not kept. Fighting broke out again and again.

When gold was discovered in Montana, troops were sent to keep open the Bozeman Trail, a path to the mines. These troops set up military posts right in the middle of the Sioux hunting ground. The Indians, led by Red Cloud, again fought to protect their lands. At last, in 1868, a treaty was signed, the Bozeman Trail was closed, and the forts were destroyed. That same year the Shoshone, led by Chief Washakie, agreed to move to the Wind River Reservation.

But the Indians who had been forced onto reservations refused to stay there. White men invaded the Black Hills, which were an important part of Indian tradition. Fighting began again. In 1876, Dull Knife, Crazy Horse, Two Moons, and Sitting Bull made one last try to keep their land at the Little Bighorn River. They won the battle. They defeated Colonel George Armstrong Custer. But white reaction to "Custer's Last Stand" was so violent that it signaled the beginning of the end of Indian hopes for the future in Wyoming. By 1877, the Indians

Chief Red Cloud led the Sioux in a fight against the invasion of their lands.

were permanently defeated and herded onto reservations.

In the meantime, white settlement in Wyoming was growing. Gold was discovered at South Pass and that brought in several thousand miners. After the building of the Union Pacific Railroad across the state in 1867-1868, the territory of Wyoming was created. The territorial government was formed in April 1868. In December of the following year, the territory of Wyoming made a perma-

nent mark on the history of the world.

At that time, there were few places on the planet where women had any say in government. Abigail Adams had warned her husband John—one of the creators of the United States Constitution—that women would not put up with being ruled by men much longer. But even the land of the free—the government of the people, by the people, and for the people—would not allow women the right to vote.

At left, Custer poses in a buckskin hunting outfit for a St. Louis photographer. Below, Indians camp outside a U.S. Army outpost.

Wyoming was the first state to give women the right to vote. Above, a scene at the Cheyenne polls in 1888.

In Wyoming, women had struggled across the country by covered wagon. They worked side by side with their husbands on farms and ranches. They risked death by starvation, exposure, and disease. And to the men in the territorial legislature, it just made sense that they should have the right to vote. On December 10, 1869, Wyoming women became the first women in this country—and most of the world—to gain that right. Women in the rest of the country would have to wait until 1920.

In 1889, a constitutional convention was held at Cheyenne, and, in 1890, Wyoming became the 44th state in the Union.

At first, there weren't many farmers in Wyoming. There were ranchers. The rolling plains were perfect for cattle. There was plenty of grass for them to eat, and the grass lasted through the winter. Pretty soon, the great cattle drives brought herds up from Texas to graze on the Wyoming range.

But there were problems. Too many cattle were brought in. They overcrowded the range. Rustlers began to raid the herds. And then the winter of 1887 hit. Temperatures dropped so low that one-sixth of the cattle died from lack of water and food. Many ranches closed. The ranchers who stayed began to be more careful.

Then the homesteaders came in. When Wyoming belonged to the Indians, it was open land. No one person or tribe owned any particular part of it. It was a hunting ground that was shared by all. After the United States took the land from the Indians, it remained open. Ranchers built houses to live in, but the range belonged to everyone.

With the homesteaders, it was different. Under the Homestead Act of 1862, they came to claim pieces of land on which to build farms. They built fences around fields and waterholes. The range was no longer open.

Of course, the ranchers did not accept this. They fought against

Below, armed men hired by cattle growers to force homesteaders off the range during Johnson County War.

American Heritage Center, University of Wyoming

the homesteaders. Sometimes there was violence. In 1892, ranchers and farmers battled each other in the Johnson County War. When it was over, the open range was gone. Fences went up around ranches as well as farms.

There were also fights when sheep were brought into the area. The cattle ranchers did not want sheep on their range. They claimed that cattle wouldn't go where sheep had been. They said that sheep destroyed the range and poisoned the waterholes. Some cattlemen became violent. Shepherds were killed and herds of sheep destroyed. But eventually the ranchers discovered that cattle and sheep could be raised together, and some ranchers owned both.

From about 1900 to 1910, the the population of Wyoming grew quickly. People came to mine coal, build railroads, herd sheep, and farm the land. But Wyoming never became crowded. After 1910, its population grew more slowly and, by 1960, growth almost stopped. In the 1970s, Wyoming had less industry than any other state. And by that time,

Joel W. Rogers

A derelict cabin (above) remains from frontier days. At right, the railroad reaches Wyoming.

people were beginning to think that wasn't such a bad thing.

Other states—states which had grown faster—were starting to look a little shabby. Their water and air were polluted. Their forests were cut down. Their hills and mountains were dotted with houses.

But Wyoming was different. Wyoming remained clean, wild, and beautiful.

It still is.

A Wyoming Childhood

"I know the snow was deeper then than it is now because we could tunnel. The woodpile was just up the hill and we would shoot the wood down the snow tunnel . . . . We had an outside door to the basement where our furnace was. That's the way we got it (the wood) in."

Edith Brown and Thelma Fontenelle have lived all their lives on a Wyoming ranch. They have many shared memories of life on four thousand acres of cattle land. They also remember when a bunch of Norwegians and Swedes came to chop down trees for railroad ties. They were called tie-hacks and the place where they lived with their families was called the tie-camp.

"We had this little green schoolhouse down here . . . just a little old tiny cabin. And we had eighteen kids in it when they were building the flume."

"Always before we only had three or four kids, you know."

"Oh, we thought they were pretty fancy because they didn't wear long underwear like we did."

"We just envied them no end 'cause we—our folks dressed us warm, you

At right, Edith Brown and Thelma Fontenelle. In the background is the Scandinavian flume.

Photos by Michael Reagan

know, which meant we had to wear long underwear. And when the spring would come . . ."

". . . We could have our underwear rolled up to go down the road after we left Mother. We would roll our under-

wear up and go down there because we were pretty envious of these tie-camp kids."

The flume Thelma mentioned was an amazing thing. The tie and timber company needed a way to move the wood. So they built a kind of water slide *nine miles long!*

The two sisters also remember the men who worked for the tie and timber company. They especially remember one man who used to break up log jams.

"There was old Bradey. That was the dynamiter. And he had dynamited so long that his equilibrium was shot. And he walked real strange. And we used to be so afraid that he—when he set the dynamite off—that he'd never get out of the way. But he always did. And he loved classical music. So he sent to Sweden and got a lot of classical records and we had an old fashioned phonograph and he would come and play his classical music."

Good memories to have on a cold Wyoming night when the air is clear and the stars are bright and the nearest neighbor is a long, long way away.

Cattle graze within sight of the mountains.

Lost Springs Wins

"Lost Springs isn't very large, that you know. There's three or six or nine people who live here. But there's three or six or nine people who live any-where in this America. And I think it is very important that these people have a right to preserve their way of life."

The history of the railroads in the West is an interesting one. In lots of places, there were railroad tracks before there were people. The railroad companies adver-tised to bring settlers onto the land.

To encourage the railroads to build, the federal government gave them a lot of rights and privi-leges, which they used. But recent-ly someone challenged the rail-roads in Wyoming . . . and won.

The woman was Leda Price. She's mayor of a town that has maybe nine people living in it. When the railroad wanted to raise its embankment so that travelers wouldn't be able to see Lost Springs from the road or cross the tracks to buy some-thing from the store, Mayor Price knew Lost Springs was lost. Unless she could stop the rail-road. Unless she could convince the courts that Lost Springs was worth saving.

"Why not preserve it? You'd look back years later and say, why did I let it go down the drain? It was incorpo-rated in 1911, and I don't think we have the right to do that. I don't think anybody has the right to do that."

The question really is this: is a town more than a wide spot in the road? What would it mean to

Max Aguilera-Hellweg

people to know that the town where they were born and raised no longer existed?

"My dad came out here and homesteaded in 1908. From Kansas. Prierview, Kansas. And then 1909, he brought the immigrant car and my mother and my two brothers out. And he had a top buggy and a team of mules and a few things to go along the farm and we lived seven miles southeast of here.

Small memories of a small town. A sense of belonging together, or belonging to a place on this earth.

"Basically, the judge has told the railroad that the way of life in Lost Springs was worth preserving and that the railroad could not run rampant over the town of Lost Springs."

Lost Springs won.

Lost Springs mayor Leda Price is pictured below.

The Rich Earth

Wyoming is a young state, just about a century old. It has not moved far from its beginnings in the land. Little more than a hundred years ago, the Indians of Wyoming found everything they needed in the earth or on the plains. Today, the people of Wyoming still look to the land for their living.

In the middle of the last century, there were important gold and coal mines in Wyoming. Today, the mineral that fuels the state's economy is oil. About $3 billion worth of oil is pumped out of the earth every year. When you add Wyoming's other minerals, the total accounts for more than a third of the state's income. Some of those minerals are coal, natural gas, trona, clay, gemstones, sand, gypsum, and uranium. Wyoming is

The Pathfinder uranium mine.

Above, grazing beef cattle. Below, sheep are docked for springtime shearing in Buffalo.

they set the pattern for Wyoming agriculture. Agriculture accounts for a fairly small percentage of the state's income, but it is a very important part of the economy. And most of the agriculture in Wyoming is ranching. Cattle is still king in this state where cowboys once rode the open range—both beef and dairy cattle. But sheep have taken their place in the economy, too. Wyoming is the nation's third largest sheep and wool producer. The cattlemen and the sheepmen have not only made friends. They're often the same people.

second only to New Mexico in uranium production.

Compared to most states, Wyoming doesn't have a lot of manufacturing. You won't find rows of factories belching out clouds of black smoke. There are factories, of course, but they are less important to the economy than in any other state besides Alaska. And most of Wyoming's factories process the resources of the land. There are chemical factories, food processing plants, and sawmills.

When cattle drivers pushed the great herds up from Texas,

There are field crops grown in Wyoming. Most of them are grown on irrigated land. They include sugar beets and barley, corn, wheat, and hay. The dry farms grow hay, wheat, and other grains. Just about all of the hay is grown to feed Wyoming's cattle.

There's one more way in which the land is important to Wyoming's economy. People come to look at it. Those millions of tourists who come to gaze at Old Faithful and camp in the mountains also spend money. They bring in about three-quarters of a billion dollars every year.

The land is still taking good care of the people of Wyoming.

Yellowstone's geysers (above) attract tourists to Wyoming. Below, a harvest of sugar beets.

A Big Job

"This is the truck that I spend eight hours a day in five days a week out here at Cordero Mining Company. You've seen it and you can tell it is just almost unbelievable. It's so big. It feels like you are driving an apartment house."

Most people have never even seen a truck as big as the one Marilyn Boone drives every working day. And most of those trucks are not driven by women.

"When my husband was alive, he used to get a big kick out of the fact that I drove this truck. We would be out in public somewhere and I would be all dolled up in my velvet jacket and skirt and all this, that, and the other and he'd say, 'Do you know what this lady does for a living?' And then he would pull out a picture of me beside my truck out here."

But Marilyn did not go after her job as a truck driver so that she could surprise people. She just wanted better pay than she

At right and above, Marilyn Boone Gragg poses with the truck she operates at the Cordero mine.

was getting as a secretary. So she applied for the job and got it. But that wasn't the end of it.

"There was quite a bit of 'Oh, my goodness, this lady can't do this,' because they'd seen me walking around as a secretary and being a miss priss and all that and the other and they really didn't think I could handle it. And it made me very determined to show everyone that I could. And I had a rather rough learning period and they did, too."

But everyone survived Marilyn's training. She's been on the job for years. But she still remembers what people said to her when she started out.

"When I first decided to come to the pit from the secretarial pool, a lot of the administrative people made the remark to me, 'But you'll get so dirty.' And of all the things that they could have thought of to object to, I thought that was the silliest that I could think of. So my standard reply was, 'But with the good salary that I am making, I can buy a lot of soap.'"

At right, a scene of coal mining at the Cordero Mining Company in Gillette. A leading coal state, Wyoming accounts for sixteen percent of total U.S. coal production.

Cordero Mining Co.

Art West

A little over 500,000 people live in Wyoming. That's about as many as live in a good-sized city—Denver, for example, or Oklahoma City. And yet, Wyoming has more than fifty museums!

Most of Wyoming's museums relate to the state's history, its heritage as part of the old West.

There's the Whitney Gallery of Western Art at the Buffalo Bill Historical Center in Cody. The Whitney Gallery has a fine collection of work by western artists like Frederic Remington, Charles Russell, and Albert Bierstadt. These are artists known around the world for their realistic and often stirring images of life in the old West.

Many of the other museums in Wyoming are historical

"Where Great Herds Come to Drink." Detail of a C.M. Russell oil painting at the Whitney Gallery.

Wyoming's greatest artworks are the creations of nature. Above, bears in Yellowstone. At the top of the right-hand page is Oxbow Bend.

museums. Their exhibits include items owned and made by pioneers and Indians. There are also collections of old photographs taken when the West was wild.

But Wyoming culture does not live only in the past. The Wyoming Arts Council and the Wyoming Artists Association see to that. The Wyoming Artists Association, for example, sponsors art shows in small towns around the state, and the Arts Council sponsors various arts activities.

Cheyenne has a civic symphony and chorus and Casper

Below, Jackson Hole's Grand Teton Music Festival. Above, Wyoming Indian traditional culture.

has a civic orchestra.

And yet, for all that, Wyoming is really a place for nature more than art. It's difficult for a sculptor to compete with the Grand Tetons—spectacular mountains that jut almost straight up out of the plain. Most paintings pale beside the sensational beauty of Yellowstone National Park. One-seventh of the land in Wyoming is national forest, with graceful lakes among the trees.

Wyoming, in a way, is one huge museum of nature's most wonderful works of art.

Basque herders with their sheep. In spring, sheep are brought in for shearing.

From Mountains to Mountains

"The first Basque that came here in 1904 in Johnson County was my greatuncle. You know, back home he would say, that is a nice country here. Why don't you come over? In those days there was no fences, no highways, just open country. Wide open country."

There is a place in the mountains between France and Spain. In that place lives a people with a proud history. They don't speak French and they don't speak Spanish. And the language they

Photos by Simon Iberlin

do speak is different from any other language we know about. They are called Basques.

The Basques are good sheep-herders. The Basques who came to Wyoming came to herd sheep. The life of a shepherd can be very lonely. And the life of a shepherd in a strange land can be even lonelier.

"They took me there to a sheep wagon. There was a bedroll. And then they tell me, 'Here is your horse. Here is your dog. There is your wagon. This is your barrel, fifty gallon barrel with water in it. And here is your sheep. Good-bye.' You can believe it."

What does a young Basque do alone on a mountain in Wyoming? How does he feel?

"You don't know what to do, what to say. You don't have nobody to talk

Michael Reagan

to in the first place. You got radio and you turn the radio on and it is in English. You don't know English. Everything was all different. The way of living, the food. And the—to be honest with you—the first at least six months of a year, I hated it."

Today there is a strong Basque community in Wyoming. It's not so lonely anymore.

"Now after all, they change everything here when we acquainted the American girls. We marry then and now we make our home. We like. We happy here."

The words may not be perfect English. But the meaning is perfectly clear.

A sheep wagon is pictured below. The wagon is home for the herder during the long months spent in the mountains with his sheep.

Beautifully Slow

There was a time when the population of Wyoming grew like wild fire. It was right after the turn of the century, from about 1900 to 1910. The number of people living in this western state grew from just over ninety thousand to almost one hundred and fifty thousand in those ten years.

And then things slowed down.

For the next fifty years, the population in Wyoming grew at about the same rate as the country as a whole. For a state, that was discouraging. And then, in the 1960s, the population stopped growing at all.

Some people were very concerned. They wanted their state to join in the economic progress of the country. They wanted to stop shipping raw materials out of the state and build their

A weathered barn stands against the Wyoming sky.

own factories. They wanted industry. They wanted Wyoming to grow.

But then something happened. People all over the country began to worry about factories and the dirt they were creating. People began to wish they had not destroyed their forests and polluted their rivers in the name of progress. They wanted things to slow down.

And there was Wyoming. Still beautiful, still wild, still full of the wonders of nature, Wyoming began to look very good. What people in the other states wanted, Wyoming still had.

What people all over the country are looking for, Wyoming still—very beautiful—is.

A Bighorn sheep in Yellowstone National Park.

Important Historical Events in Wyoming

1743 Vérendrye brothers may have come to the Bighorn Mountains from North Dakota.

1807 John Colter, a member of the Lewis and Clark party who stayed behind, entered Wyoming and probably visited Yellowstone.

1811 The Astorians cross the Bighorn Mountains and the Continental Divide.

1812 Robert Stuart and his group build the first European-style building in the state.

1824 The Rocky Mountain Fur Company under William Ashley and Andrew Henry announces discovery of the South Pass, which had already been discovered by Robert Stuart.

1832 Captain Benjamin L. E. Bonneville builds Fort Bonneville, the first fur fort in Wyoming, on the Green River.

1834 Robert Campbell and William Sublette build Fort Laramie, the first permanent white settlement in Wyoming, at the junction where the Platte and Laramie rivers cross.

1835 Samuel Parker and Marcus Whitman attend the Grand Rendezvous on the Green River, at which Parker preaches the first Protestant sermon in the Rockies.

1842 Jim Bridger builds Fort Bridger on Black Forks of the Green River. John C. Frémont leads the first government expedition into the area.

1843 Marcus Whitman brings the first large group of farming settlers over the Oregon Trail to Wyoming.

1849 The United States government buys Fort Laramie.

1851 The Great Treaty Council meets at Fort Laramie.

1854 Grattan's Massacre.

1863 Walter W. DeLacy enters Yellowstone Park.

1866 Fetterman Disaster.

1868 The Shoshone are put on the Wind River Reservation. The Union Pacific Railroad crosses Wyoming. Congress creates the Wyoming Territory out of parts of the Dakota, Utah, and Idaho territories.

1868 The Long Trail from Texas is opened.

1872 Yellowstone Park is established.

1873 The Stock Association of Laramie is organized.

1876 Battle of the Little Bighorn.

1877 Chief Washakie of the Shoshone allows the Arapaho to stay at Wind River until a reservation is arranged for them.

1879 The Stock Association of Laramie becomes the Wyoming Stock Growers' Association.

1885 The first of three bad winters causes large cattle losses. Homesteaders begin to move onto the open range.

1890 Wyoming becomes the 44th state.

1892 The Johnson County War.

1909 Five cattlemen go to prison for killing two sheep men.

1943 President Franklin D. Roosevelt creates Jackson Hole National monument.

Wyoming Almanac

Nickname. The Equality State.

Capital. Cheyenne.

State Bird. Meadowlark.

State Flower. Indian paintbrush.

State Tree. Cottonwood.

State Motto. Equal Rights.

State Song. Wyoming.

State Abbreviations. Wyo. (traditional); WY (postal).

Statehood. July 10, 1890, the 44th state.

Government. Congress: U.S. senators, 2; U.S. representatives, 1. **State Legislature:** senators, 30; representatives, 64. **Counties:** 23.

Area. 97,914 sq. mi. (253,596 sq. km.), 9th in size among the states.

Greatest Distances. north/south, 275 mi. (443 km.); east/west, 365 mi. (587 km.).

Elevation. Highest: Gannett Peak, 13,804 ft. (4,208 m). **Lowest:** Belle Fourche River, 3,100 ft. (945 m).

Population. 1980 Census: 470,816 (42% increase over 1970), 49th among the states. **Density:** 5 persons per sq. mi. (2 persons per sq. km.). **Distribution:** 63% urban, 37% rural. **1970 Census:** 332,416.

Economy. Agriculture: wheat, beans, barley, oats, sugar beets, hay, beef cattle, sheep. **Manufacturing:** petroleum products, food products, wood products, stone, clay and glass products. **Mining:** petroleum, uranium, clay, cement, lime, sand and gravel, sodium carbonate.

Places to Visit

Devils Tower National Monument, in northeastern Wyoming.

Fort Laramie National Historic Site, near Fort Laramie.

Grand Teton National Park, in northwestern Wyoming.

Hell's Half Acre, near Casper.

Wind River Canyon, near Thermopolis.

Yellowstone National Park, in northwestern Wyoming.

Annual Events

Jubilee Days in Laramie (July).

Indian Sun Dances in Ethete and Fort Washakie (July).

Frontier Days in Cheyenne (July).

Central Wyoming Fair and Rodeo in Casper (July or August).

Fine Arts Festival in Jackson Hole (July and August).

Indian pageant in Thermopolis (August).

Wyoming State Fair in Douglas (August or September).

Wyoming Counties

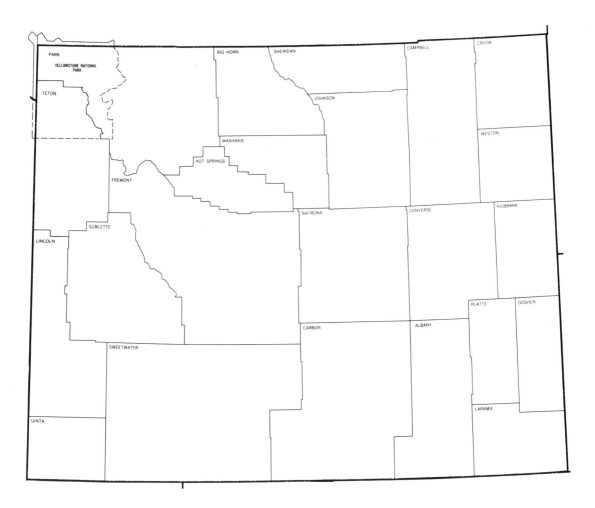

PARK

YELLOWSTONE NATIONAL
PARK

TETON

BIG HORN

SHERIDAN

CAMPBELL

CROOK

JOHNSON

WESTON

WASHAKIE

HOT SPRINGS

FREMONT

NATRONA

CONVERSE

NIOBRARA

SUBLETTE

LINCOLN

PLATTE

GOSHEN

CARBON

ALBANY

SWEETWATER

LARAMIE

UINTA

INDEX

Adams, Abigail, 15
Adams, John, 15
agriculture, 28
American Fur Company, 10, 12
Arapaho Indians, 9
Ashley, William, 11
Astor, John Jacob, 10
Bannock Indians, 9
Basques, 38-41
Blackfeet Indians, 9
Bozeman Trail, 14
Bridger Pass, 12
Campbell, Robert, 12
Cheyenne Indians, 9
Clark, William, 9-10
Colter, John, 10
Crazy Horse, Chief, 14
Crow Indians, 9
culture (of Wyoming), 35-37
Custer, George Armstrong, 14
Dull Knife, Chief, 14
economy (of Wyoming), 27-29
Fort Laramie, 12
"Forty-Niners," 13
Frémont, John C., 13
gold, 13, 14
Great Treaty Council (1851), 13
history (of Wyoming), 8-19, 45
Homestead Act of 1862, 17
homesteaders, 17-18
Indians, 9, 13-14, 17, 27
industry, 18
Johnson County War, 18
Lee, Daniel, 12

Lee, Jason, 12
Lewis, Meriwether, 9-10
Little Bighorn River, 14
oil, 27
Oregon Trail, 13
Overland Trail, 12-13
Pony Express, 13
population, 18, 43
ranching, 17, 18
Red Cloud, Chief, 14
Rocky Mountain Fur Company, 11
Sacagawea, 10
sheep, 18
Shoshone Indians, 9
Sioux Indians, 9
Sitting Bull, Chief, 14
South Pass, 11, 12, 14
statehood, 16
Stuart, Robert, 11
Sublette, William, 12
tourism, 29
Two Moons, Chief, 14
Union Pacific Railroad, 14
Washakie, Chief, 14
Whitman, Marcus, 13
Whitney Gallery, 35
Wilson Hunt Price expedition, 10-11
Wind River Reservation, 14
women's rights, 15-16
women's suffrage, 16
Wyoming Artists Association, 36
Wyoming Arts Council, 36
Yellowstone Park, 10
Young, Brigham, 13